READY STEADY GO

Wheels

Barbara Taylor

Illustrated by Jane Carroll

KINGFISHER BOOKS

Contents

Wheels

Kingfisher Books, Grisewood & Dempsey Ltd,
Elsley House, 24–30 Great Titchfield Street, London W1P 7AD

First published in paperback in 1991 by Kingfisher Books
10 9 8 7 6 5 4 3 2 1
Originally published in hardback in 1990 by Kingfisher Books

BRITISH LIBRARY CATALOGUING IN PUBLICATION DATA
Taylor, Barbara
Wheels
1. Wheels
I. Title II. Carroll, Jane III. Series
531'.8
ISBN 0 86272 863 0

Edited by Jackie Dobbyne
Designed by Monica Chia
Cover design by Pinpoint Design Company
Phototypeset by Southern Positives and Negatives (SPAN),
Lingfield, Surrey
Colour separations by Scantrans Pte Ltd, Singapore
Printed in Spain

Wheels Everywhere

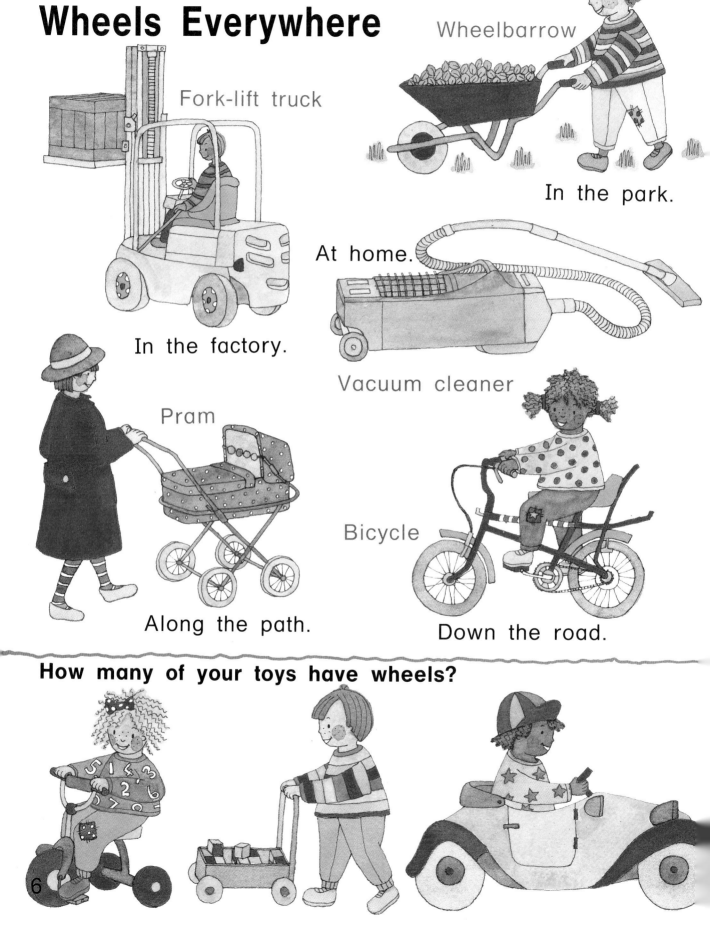

Fork-lift truck

In the factory.

Wheelbarrow

In the park.

At home.

Vacuum cleaner

Pram

Along the path.

Bicycle

Down the road.

How many of your toys have wheels?

Tractor

Car

In the street.

On the farm.

Trolley

In the supermarket.

Train

On the railway tracks.

How Many Wheels?

1 wheel

Steering wheel

2 wheels   Tandem

3 wheels   4 wheels   Roller skate

Scooter

6 wheels   8 wheels

Helicopter   Buggy

Aeroplane

) wheels

rticulated lorry

3 wheels

You can't see all the wheels in this drawing.
There are 9 wheels each side of the lorry.

Road train

wheels

There are 17 wheels each side of this
road train.

ow many wheels are there here?   Car transporter   9

Big Wheels, Small Wheels

Some things have big wheels.

Paddle steamer

Ferris wheel

Some things have big and small wheels.

Chopper

Tractor

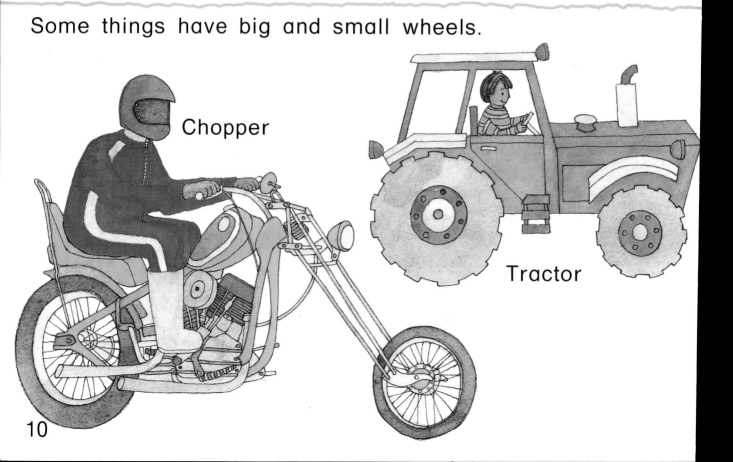

Some things have small wheels.

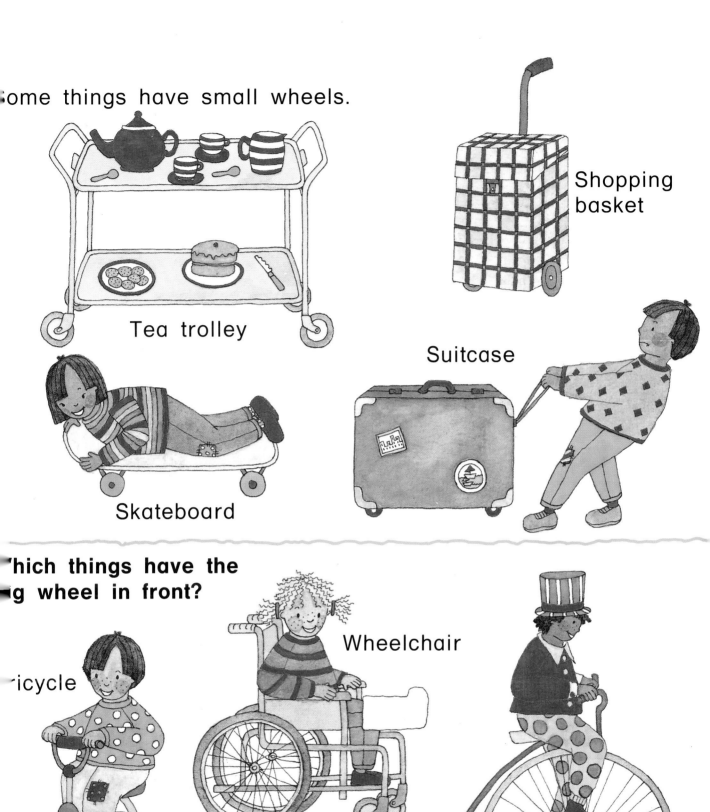

Tea trolley

Shopping basket

Skateboard

Suitcase

Which things have the big wheel in front?

Tricycle

Wheelchair

Penny-farthing

Which things have the small wheel in front?

11

Giant Wheels

Tractor scrapers have huge wheels.

hey scrape away the bumps to make roads flat.

Building a Road

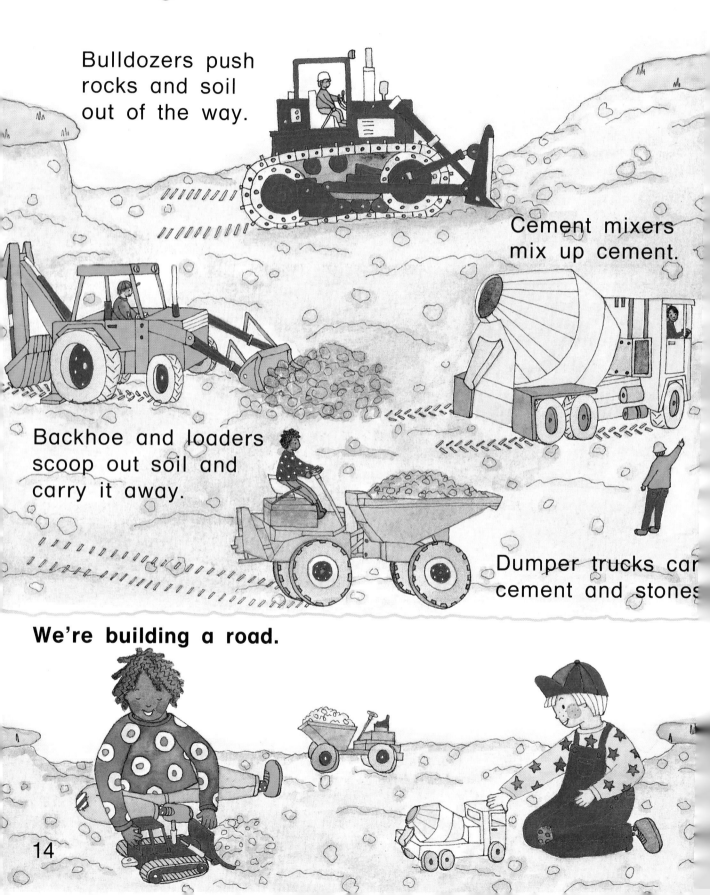

Bulldozers push rocks and soil out of the way.

Cement mixers mix up cement.

Backhoe and loaders scoop out soil and carry it away.

Dumper trucks car cement and stones

We're building a road.

14

Road rollers press the tar
to make it flat and smooth.

Tip-up trucks tip out stones.

ad finishers
ead tar and
vel.

an you see which machines we're using?

Going Places

Wheels help people to travel more easily. They carry us to school, to work, to the shops and on holiday.
What's your favourite way to travel?

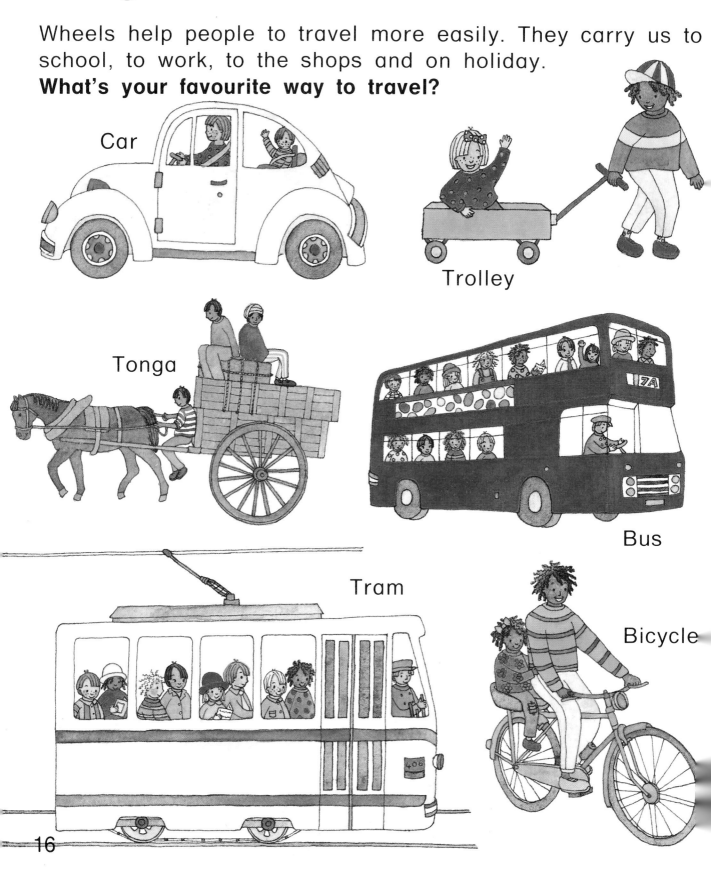

Car

Trolley

Tonga

Bus

Tram

Bicycle

Train

Autorickshaw

Buggy

Gypsy caravan

Coach

Chair lift

17

Helping People

Police cars speed to
the scene of the crime.

Traffic motorcycles
patrol the motorways.

Ambulances take sick people to hospital.

Fire engine
put out fire

We're dressing up as helpers.

18

Breakdown trucks pick up broken-down cars.

Wheelchairs help people who cannot walk easily.

Street carts clean up litter.

Refuse trucks collect rubbish.

Can you match us to the helpers in the picture?

19

Carrying Loads

Wheels help us to carry heavy loads and deliver urgent parcels.

Fork-lift truck

Pick-up truck

Estate car

Despatch rider

Petrol tanker

Can you find these loads in the picture?

Envelope

Lamp

Bale of stra

Bricks

Plant

Horse box

Tractor and trailor

Removals van

Florist's van

Delivery van

Ladder

Suitcase

Horse

Pane of glass

Pulley Wheels

A pulley wheel has a groove around the edge. A rope or cable fits into the groove. Pulley wheels help us to lift heavy things.

How many of your toys have pulley wheels?

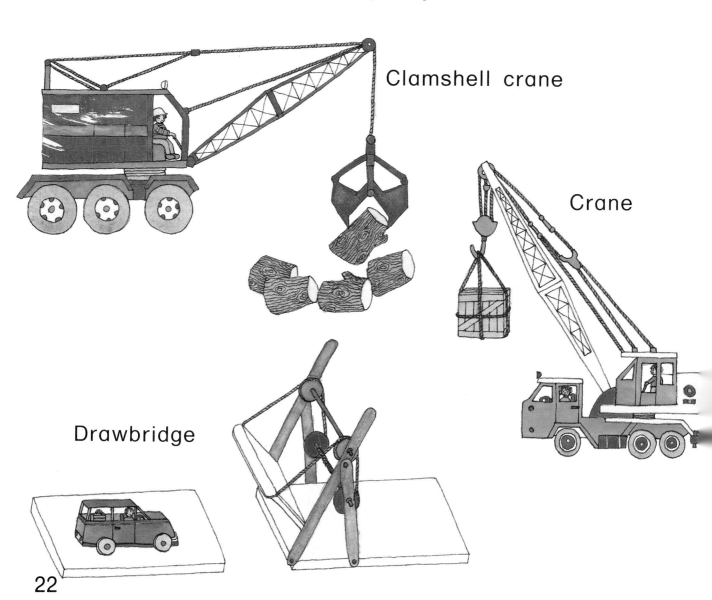

Clamshell crane

Crane

Drawbridge

22

Gear Wheels

A gear wheel has teeth along
the edge. The teeth of one
gear wheel fit inside the teeth
of another gear wheel. When
one gear wheel turns it makes
the others turn too.

Can you find these gear wheels in your home?

Egg whisk

Drill

Can opener

Remember to mind
the sharp edges!

What Makes Wheels Work?

Wheels need energy to make them work.

Roller skates

Lawn mower

Hand

Bicycle wheel

Feet

Electricit

Water

Toy

Battery

Water wheel

Can you make a windmill?

24

Pony

Cart

Steam

Train

Van

Petrol

Car

Diesel

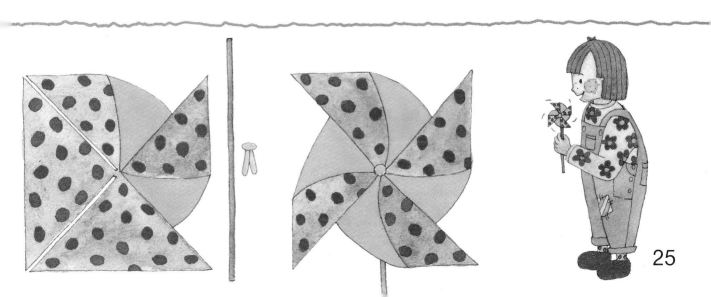

25

Wheels for Sport

Sports cars and bikes have special wheels to help them win races. Wide wheels help to grip the road better and thin wheels are easier to turn.

Racing car

Road racer

Kart

Racing bike

We're playing with our racing cars.

Trials bike

Motocross bike

Rally car

Dragster

Who do you think will win this race?

Wheels for Fun

Which is your favourite wheel?

Roundabout in the playground.

Unicycle at
the circus.

Playbus in the park.

Train at the zoo.

Toy duck in
the garden.

Beach buggy on the sand.

Merry-go-round at the fair.

Roller coaster at
the theme park.

Catherine wheel at
the fireworks party.

Wheel Tracks

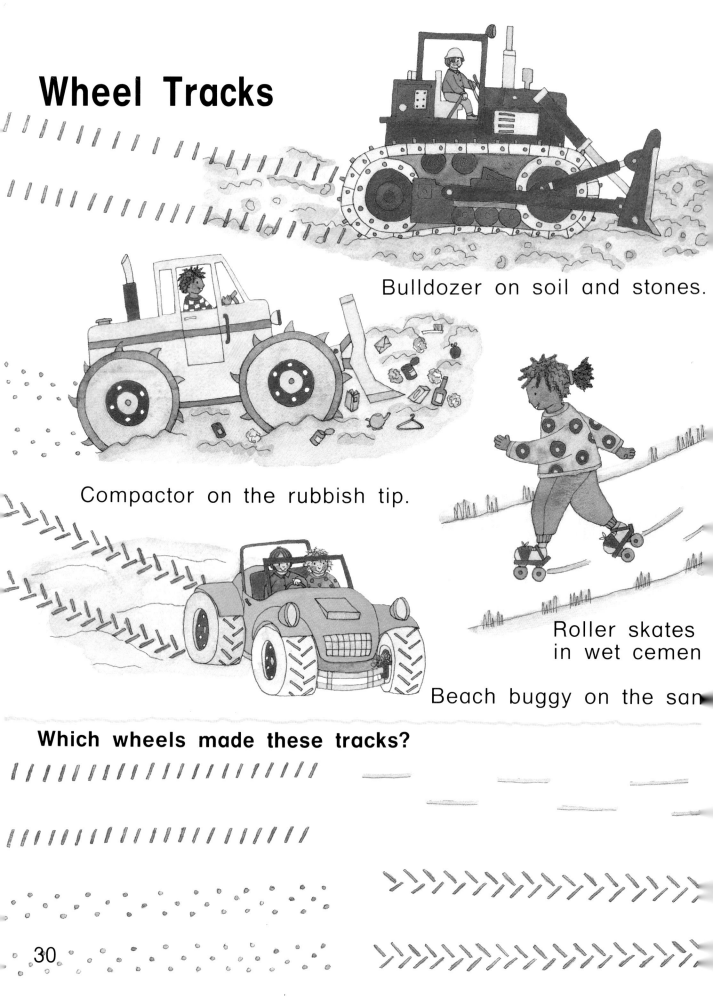

Bulldozer on soil and stones.

Compactor on the rubbish tip.

Roller skates
in wet cemen

Beach buggy on the san

Which wheels made these tracks?

Road roller on sticky tar.

Wheelbarrow in the garden.

Horse and wagon on muddy road.

Snow plough in soft snow.

How many vehicles can you see on the road?

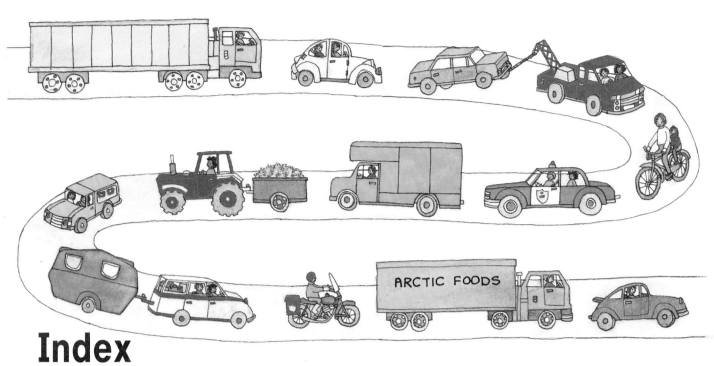

Index

You can find out more about wheels on the pages listed below.

> If you look closely at the picture above, you will find an articulated lorry, a car, a breakdown truck and a broken-down car, a bicycle, a police car, a removals van, a tractor and trailer, a delivery van, an estate car and caravan, a motorcycle, a refrigerated lorry and a sports car.